1922: The Wendell Phillips High School heavyweight basketball team wins title in the Chicago Public High School League.

1926: A group of Wendell Phillips players become part of a traveling team called South Side Giles Post of the American Legion.*

1927: The South Side Giles Post team becomes the Savoy Big Five. Some of the players join the Tommy Brookins Globe Trotters team.*

1927: With manager Abe Saperstein, Walter "Toots" Wright, William "Kid" Oliver, Byron "Fat" Long, Albert "Runt" Pullins, and Andy Washington become the New York Harlem Globe Trotters. In their first season, they win nearly every game.*

1929: Inman "Big Jack" Jackson joins the team.*

1929–1939: The Great Depression.

1930s: The Harlem Globetrotters begin performing ballhandling tricks during games.*

1937: The National Basketball League (NBL) is founded.

1941: Reece "Goose" Tatum joins the Globetrotters.*

1942: Bob Karstens becomes the first white player to sign a contract to play for the Globetrotters.

1946: The Basketball Association of America (BAA) is founded.

1946: Marques Haynes and Boid Buie join the Globetrotters.*

There's an ongoing debate between several sources about the exact timing of the above starred events and the roster of the "first official" Harlem Globe Trotter team.

April 15, 1947: Jackie Robinson becomes the first African American to play in a Major League Baseball game.

February 19, 1948: The Globetrotters beat the Minnesota Lakers, 61–59.

July 1948: Nat "Sweetwater" Clifton joins the Globetrotters.

1949: The Basketball Association of America (BAA) and the National Basketball League (NBL) merge to create the National Basketball Association (NBA).

1950: Production of *The Harlem Globetrotters* movie begins.

January 1, 1950: The Harlem Globetrotters are invited to play in the famous Madison Square Garden for the first time. They beat the New York Celtics, 75–60.

April 2, 1950: The Globetrotters play their first game in the "World Series of Basketball" against the College All-Stars.

April 25, 1950: The owner of the Boston Celtics selects Charles "Chuck" Cooper as his second-round draft pick, and the Washington Capitols also select two African American players: Earl Lloyd and Harold Hunter.

May 3, 1950: The Globetrotters make their first European trip and play in nine countries: Portugal, Switzerland, England, Belgium, Germany, Italy, Morocco, Algeria, and France.

(Timeline continues on page 38.)

ABOUT THIS BOOK
The illustrations for this book were created digitally
in Clip Studio Paint Pro and Photoshop.
This book was edited by Deirdre Jones and
designed by Saho Fujii and Christine Kettner.
The production was supervised by Patricia Alvarado,
and the production editor was Annie McDonnell.
The text was set in Franklin Gothic ITC Demi,
and the display type is Highway.
Little, Brown and Company
Hachette Book Group
1290 Avenue of the Americas,
New York, NY 10104
Visit us at LBYR.com
First Edition: November 2020

Little, Brown and Company
is a division of Hachette Book Group, Inc.
The Little, Brown name and logo are trademarks
of Hachette Book Group, Inc.
The publisher is not responsible for websites
(or their content)
that are not owned by the publisher.
Library of Congress Cataloging-in-Publication Data
Names: Slade, Suzanne, author. | Tate, Don, illustrator. |
Little, Brown and Company.
Title: Swish! : the slam-dunking, alley-ooping,
high-flying Harlem Globetrotters / written by Suzanne Slade ;
illustrated by Don Tate.
Other titles: Harlem Globetrotters
Description: First Edition. | New York : Little, Brown and Company, [2020] |
Includes webography. | Audience: Ages: 4–8.
Identifiers: LCCN 2019022193 | ISBN 9780316481670 (hardcover) |
Subjects: LCSH: Harlem Globetrotters—History—Juvenile literature. |
African American basketball players—Biography—Juvenile literature. |
Basketball players—United States—Biography—Juvenile literature. |
Discrimination in sports—United States—Juvenile literature. |
National Basketball Association—History—Juvenile literature. |
Basketball—United States—
History—Juvenile literature. | Illustrated children's books.
Classification: LCC GV885.52.H37 S53 2020 |
DDC 796.323/64097471—dc23
LC record available at https://lccn.loc.gov/2019022193
ISBN: 978-0-316-48167-0 (hardcover)

PRINTED IN CHINA
1010
10 9 8 7 6 5 4 3 2 1

SWISH!

THE SLAM-DUNKING, ALLEY-OOPING, HIGH-FLYING HARLEM GLOBETROTTERS

WRITTEN BY
SUZANNE SLADE

ILLUSTRATED BY
DON TATE

LITTLE, BROWN AND COMPANY
New York   Boston

IT ALL STARTED WITH THOSE BOYS

*thump-thump*ing basketballs
up and down Chicago's South Side
in alleys, driveways, and parking lots.
Raw talent and determination in worn-out sneakers
practicing **nonstop layups**,
all-net free throws,
and **sky-high jump shots.**

When their team charged into Wendell Phillips High
wearing those official school jerseys,
every student grew an inch taller with pride.
Their players were unstoppable—division champs!

Everyone could see they had as much talent
as the country's best hoopsters.
But the top teams only recruited white players.
So after graduation, those Wendell Phillips stars
joined traveling teams for black players.

Before long, a few players met a small man with a big dream,
Abe Saperstein, who helped them form their own team—
the Harlem Globetrotters.
The name sounded grand—like they'd played all over the world!
Well, not quite. But they barnstormed their way across America,
Little Abe and five giant players—**Toots Wright**, **Kid Oliver**,
Fat Long, **Runt Pullins**, and **Andy Washington**.

They squeezed into an old Model T
and chugged from town to town,
searching for anyone who would play—
farmers, students, lumberjacks—
and people who would pay to watch.

Seven nights a week,
the road-weary team played ball
healthy, sick, or injured
and won nearly every game.
But hometown fans
didn't like out-of-town hotshots
skunking their team.

Soon, the Trotters came up with a plan.
Smack in the middle of the game,
each player performed a ballhandling trick
while the others took a short rest.
Crowds howled with delight at the surprising sights:

One-finger ball spinning.
Rapid-fire mini dribbling.
And **a ricochet head shot!**
Suddenly, people didn't mind
when the hilarious Trotters beat their team.

The Globetrotters played wherever they could:
barns, basements, even the bottom
of a dried-up swimming pool.
The crowds laughed and cheered!
But as soon as the game ended,
the cheers stopped.

The tired, hungry players
weren't always welcomed
in hotels or restaurants.
They couldn't use most gas station
restrooms or phones.
Nearly every drinking fountain
wore a "whites only" sign.

Downhearted yet determined,
a new fire fueled their game.
The Trotters would prove that all players—all people—
deserved to be treated the same.

With their **fancy footwork, fast passes,**
and **one-handed dunk shots,**
they played the most breathtaking,
groundbreaking ball the country had ever seen.

Boid Buie

Marques Haynes

Goose Tatum

Years bounced by.

Older players retired.

New ones stepped in.

Goose Tatum—the "clown prince," who rolled that ball across eighty-four inches of steel-strong arms.

Marques Haynes—a dazzling, dizzying dribbler with lightning-fast hands.

Boid Buie—a spectacular sharpshooter who had only one arm.

With their slapstick tricks and pinpoint shots,
the Trotters' game became known as "The Show."
They made the game *look* so easy,
people didn't even notice their incredible talent.
But this team was more than a show.
They were **skilled athletes**, **expert players**,
and **electrifying performers** all rolled into one—
professionals at the game.

But the professional basketball teams
didn't allow black players.
Determined to make people see their talent
instead of their skin color,
the Globetrotters challenged the best team
in the National Basketball League:
the mighty Minnesota Lakers.

What?! You could almost hear the nation gasp.

A pro team play those high-flying showboats? *How ridiculous!*

Yet the Lakers agreed.

They couldn't wait to trounce the Trotters.

Shivering fans lined up outside Chicago Stadium
in middle-of-the-night darkness
on February 19, 1948.
People across the country slapped down sure bets.
Easy money! No way the Lakers could lose.
They had a six-foot-ten giant: George Mikan.

Surrounded by a raucous, record-breaking crowd,
the Globetrotters jogged out in comical striped shorts.
But they left their tricks behind—
tonight was straight-up, serious ball.

Right from the start,

Goose stuck to Mikan like gum on a shoe.

Yet Mikan quickly scored eighteen points

and blocked every shot Goose put up.

By halftime, the Lakers were ahead.

But the Globetrotters fought back

and tied the game.

Right before the end-of-game buzzer, the Trotters sent one last shot **SOARING** toward the net.

Swish!

Globetrotters win 61–59!

Without saying a word,

the Trotters showed the world

that players with different skin colors belonged on the same court.

The Lakers demanded a rematch. The win was a fluke!

A year later, the teams faced off again.

And the Trotters won again!

Now the most popular team in America,
the Globetrotters played to sold-out stadiums
and signed a Hollywood movie contract!
Meanwhile, NBA teams were barely selling enough tickets to pay the bills.

Frustrated team owners gathered
to pick next season's recruits.
One by one, they carefully considered each athlete's talent.
And suddenly, their "whites only" rule seemed ridiculous.

Then something incredible happened.

The Celtics' owner announced
an astounding choice—
Chuck Cooper!—
one of the most remarkable players
he'd *ever* seen,
and one of the Globetrotters' newest recruits.
Soon, another owner declared his top picks:
two more phenomenal black players.

And the game was never the same.
It became **nonstop**
give-it-all-you-got,
out-to-win-it,
sky's-the-limit
basketball!

After breaking into the NBA,
the Globetrotters broke out into the world.
They played in a dusty bullring in Peru,
in a cow pasture in New Zealand,
and on a court built over barrels in Germany.

GERMANY

PERU

NEW ZEALAND

The crowds were astonished by their **slam dunks**, **alley-oops**, and other **high-flying surprises**. They made thousands of new friends, met popes, princes, and presidents, and even sipped tea with the queen of England!

They shared their joy, laughter, and warm friendship with nations around the world (even ones who weren't friends with the United States).

Back home, the Harlem Globetrotters were named
"America's Ambassadors of Goodwill."
How about that!
The team that brought black and white America closer together
brought the world a little closer together too.

And lived up to their **Globetrotter** name after all!

To Wendy, Brooke, Freddy, and Fred,
who was a guest in "The Show" —SS

To my Armadillustrators picture book critique group buddies:
Jeff C., Christopher J., Kyle M., Thomas J.,
Kevin R., and Carlos de la G. —DT

MORE ABOUT THE TROTTERS

The Harlem Globetrotters played their first game in 1927, a time when other barnstorming basketball teams also called themselves "Globe Trotters" to sound as if they'd traveled the world. (Barnstorming teams *did* travel a lot, but usually to small towns to play exhibition games.) Abe Saperstein, the Trotters' coach, originally named the team the New York Harlem Globe Trotters, after the neighborhood of Harlem in New York City. This area was the center of African American culture at the time, and Abe thought audiences would be impressed if they believed the team originated there. Within a few years, though, the team dropped "New York," which resulted in their now iconic name, the Harlem Globetrotters. Interestingly, they didn't play in Harlem until 1968.

When the Trotters started out, Abe was their coach, driver, booking manager, publicist, accountant, and occasional teammate. Even though he was only five foot three, Abe stepped in as a substitute player when needed, wearing a uniform under his suit on game days just in case. At times, however, his relationship with the players was complicated and conflicted. Many team members felt he underpaid them and didn't treat them with respect. A few players, such as Runt Pullins and Marques Haynes, became so angry with Abe that they quit the Globetrotters and formed their own teams. Some people questioned whether Abe treated the players unfairly due to the color of their skin. Despite these issues, he remained with the Globetrotters for forty years.

Soon after the team hit the road around 1927, the Great Depression hit America in 1929. People had little money and hardly any to spare for luxuries like basketball tickets. Yet the crowds that came to see the Globetrotters grew and grew. Their incredible skills and superstar popularity served as a huge catalyst for change, and by 1950, the NBA finally decided to allow black players into the league. Chuck Cooper, who had played for the Trotters during the College All-Stars tournament and was under contract to join the team, became the first African American drafted into the NBA. Earl Lloyd, the first African American to play in an NBA game, had played in a Globetrotter tour and was expected to join the Trotters full-time after college. Nat "Sweetwater" Clifton, a popular Globetrotter in the late 1940s, was the first black player to sign an NBA contract.

The Globetrotters embarked on their first trip to Europe in 1950. Although the team had faced discrimination in America for decades, they were enthusiastically welcomed (and often treated like royalty) in almost every country they visited. In 1951, a group of players headed to Argentina, a country that had a strained relationship with America. But it didn't take long for the winsome Trotters to make new friends there, which opened valuable lines of communication for the United States. That same summer, another team of Trotters visited forty-seven cities in Europe, where they made friends with government officials and thousands of fans. After impressing several important leaders in Germany, the US State Department sent the team a grateful letter that said, "The Globetrotters have proven themselves ambassadors of extraordinary good will wherever they have gone."

And that goodwill has continued. Today the Harlem Globetrotters field several teams, which perform across America and visit countries around the world. With their hilarious tricks, phenomenal talent, and warm hearts, these high-flying hoopsters break down cultural barriers and make new friends wherever they go.

ARTIST'S NOTE

A few years ago, while visiting an elementary school in Fort Worth, Texas, for their annual Author's Day, I was asked to say a few words at an early morning assembly. The gym buzzed with excitement. Students clapped, cheered, and laughed as I entered. I thought the enthusiasm was about me, until I noticed a Globetrotter standing at center court! He spun a ball on one finger. He performed other tricks. Then he swished the ball into the hoop from an impossible distance.

It was just as amazing to see as an adult as when I went to see the Globetrotters as a child. I loved when they came to my town of Des Moines, Iowa, and played at the historic Veterans Memorial Auditorium. My favorite players were Fred "Curly" Neal and Meadowlark Lemon, the closest things to black superheroes that I knew of. And while I wasn't a sports kid, that didn't stop me from trying to spin a basketball on one finger when I got home from "The Show."

Illustrating a book about the Globetrotters was an opportunity to return to the superheroes of my youth, but also presented a few challenges. There are many legends about the true origins of the team, and there were several teams that carried the Globetrotter name. To create the illustrations, I relied on photographs that ran in newspapers, programs that were handed out at games, and other publications and advertisements of the times. The biggest challenge was trying to portray the various team uniforms throughout the years, the design of which seemed to change with the wind. The black-and-white photography of the 1930s and 1940s also made it difficult to determine whether a jersey would have been blue or red. In the end, I made educated guesses based on solid research—especially when trying to determine the exact date those white-striped shorts first appeared.

Team members changed, too, and since *Swish!* is the story of a historic basketball team, and less about specific players, I didn't include numbers on jerseys to avoid identifying someone not mentioned in the text—although on the final spread, I did include Bob Karstens, one of the few white players, and Lynette Woodard, the first female player.

Most of the stories I've written and/or illustrated have been about the lives of little-known African American historical figures who have overcome great obstacles to make important contributions to our world. The Globetrotters certainly aren't unknown, but their story of hard work, perseverance, and using their talents to outshine the barriers of racial injustice sets an example for kids to live by. My hope is that *Swish!* demonstrates for children—and everyone—the heights they can reach, even when it feels like the world's against them.

SELECTED SOURCES AND CREDITS

"1950-51 SEASON OVERVIEW, NBA's Color Line Is Broken," http://archive.nba.com/history/season/19501951.html.

"*Chicago's Harlem Globetrotters*." WTTW. http://interactive.wttw.com/a/chicago-stories-harlem-globetrotters.

Green, Ben. *Spinning the Globe: The Rise, Fall, and Return to Greatness of the Harlem Globetrotters*. New York: Amistad Press, 2005 (*Source of page 36 US State Department quotation*).

Harlem Globetrotters: The Team that Changed the World. Chicago: Team Works Media, 2005. DVD.

"Minneapolis Lakers vs. Harlem Globetrotters," http://stewthornley.net/mplslakers_trotters.html.

Pruter, Robert Illinois High School Association, "Early Phillips High School Basketball Teams," https://www.ihsa.org/NewsMedia/IllinoisHStoric/IllinoisHStoricArticle.aspx?url=/archive/hstoric/basketball_phillips.htm.

Stern, Bill. *Bill Stern's Sports Book*. Vol. 2. Chicago: Ziff-Davis, 1952.

Zinkoff, Dave, and Edgar Williams. *Around the World with the Harlem Globetrotters*. Philadelphia: Macrae Smith Co, 1953.

May 24, 1950: Nat "Sweetwater" Clifton becomes the first African American player to sign an NBA contract.

1951: The Globetrotters' first trip to South America improves the United States' strained relationship with Argentina.

1951: The Globetrotters take a second trip to Europe.

August 1951: The Globetrotters play in Berlin's Olympic Stadium before seventy-five thousand fans, their largest crowd ever.

October 24, 1951: *The Harlem Globetrotters* movie releases in theaters.

May 31, 1952: The Harlem Globetrotters embark on a world tour in which they travel over fifty thousand miles and visit more than thirty nations.

January 27, 1954: *Go, Man, Go!,* a second movie featuring the Globetrotters, releases in theaters.

May 17, 1954: *Brown v. Board of Education* court ruling declares that segregated public schools are unconstitutional.

1954: Meadowlark Lemon joins the Globetrotters. He went on to play sixteen thousand games in twenty-four seasons.

1963: Fred "Curly" Neal begins his twenty-two-season career with the Globetrotters. He went on to play more than six thousand games in ninety-seven countries.

1982: The Globetrotters become the first sports team to receive a star on the Hollywood Walk of Fame.

1985: The Globetrotters sign their first female player, Lynette Woodard.

1993: Former Globetrotter player Mannie Jackson purchases the Harlem Globetrotters team and becomes the first African American to own a major international sports organization.

1996: Nelson Mandela is named an honorary member of the Globetrotters team.

2002: The Harlem Globetrotters team is inducted into the Naismith Memorial Basketball Hall of Fame in Springfield, Massachusetts.

May 2009: An official Globetrotter basketball is carried on the space shuttle *Atlantis*. The ball is now on display at the Naismith Memorial Basketball Hall of Fame.

October 18, 2011: Three Globetrotters—Kevin "Special K" Daley, Anthony "Ant" Atkinson, and Kenny "Blenda" Rodriguez—appear in a *Sesame Street* episode.

May 6, 2015: In celebration of the team's ninetieth anniversary, the Harlem Globetrotters name Pope Francis an honorary Harlem Globetrotter.

December 6, 2016: For World Trick Shot Day, Globetrotter Anthony "Buckets" Blakes makes a 583-foot-high shot from the top of the Tower of the Americas in San Antonio, Texas, into a basket on the ground.